JAMES HALL

Mindfulness Skills For Kids With Depression

Building Resilience and Self-Esteem with Proven Mindfulness Techniques

This book was professionally typeset on Reedsy.
Find out more at reedsy.com

Contents

1 Introduction   1
2 What is mindfulness?   5
3 Getting Started with Mindfulness   8
4 Understanding Emotions in Children   12
5 Mindfulness in Daily Life   17
6 Cultivating Gratitude   21
7 Managing Stress and Anxiety in Children   25
8 Building Resilience   29
9 Connecting with Others   33
10 Self-Compassion and Self-Care   37
11 Mindful Problem-Solving   41
12 Mindfulness in School   45
13 Mindful Parenting and Family Support   48
14 Overcoming obstacles   52
15 Moving Forward   56

1

Introduction

In the realm of mental health, understanding the intricate nuances of depression in children is paramount. Depression, often misconstrued as an adult-centric issue, affects children and adolescents at an alarming rate, necessitating a deeper exploration of its manifestations and implications. Concurrently, the significance of mindfulness as a therapeutic tool for bolstering mental health cannot be overstated. It is within this context that this book, "Mindfulness Skills for Kids with Depression," emerges as a beacon of hope and guidance for caregivers, educators, and mental health professionals alike. Through a comprehensive examination of depression in children, an exploration of mindfulness practices, and a delineation of the book's objectives, this introduction sets the stage for a transformative journey toward understanding and healing.

1.1 Understanding Depression in Kids

Depression in children is a multifaceted phenomenon characterized by persistent feelings of sadness, hopelessness, and a loss of interest in activities once enjoyed. Contrary to common misconceptions, depression transcends mere mood fluctuations and can significantly impede a child's emotional, social, and academic functioning. Recognizing the signs and symptoms of depression in children is crucial for early intervention and effective management. Behavioral changes, such as withdrawal from social interactions, changes in appetite or sleep patterns, and expressions of worthlessness or guilt, may serve as red flags for caregivers and educators. Moreover, understanding the underlying factors contributing to depression in children, including genetic predispositions, environmental stressors, and neurobiological factors, can inform personalized intervention strategies. By fostering an empathetic and informed approach to depression in children, caregivers and professionals can cultivate a supportive environment conducive to healing and growth.

1.2 Importance of Mindfulness for Mental Health

Mindfulness, rooted in ancient contemplative practices, has garnered increasing attention in contemporary mental health discourse for its profound therapeutic benefits. At its essence, mindfulness entails cultivating present-moment awareness with a non-judgmental attitude, allowing individuals to observe their thoughts, emotions, and bodily sensations without attachment or aversion. For children grappling with depression, mindfulness serves as a powerful tool for enhancing emotional regulation, reducing stress, and fostering resilience. Through mindfulness practices such as mindful breathing, body scans, and sensory awareness exercises, children can cultivate a greater sense of self-awareness and self-compassion, thereby mitigating the detrimental effects of depression. Moreover, research underscores the neurobiological underpinnings of mindfulness, revealing its capacity to modulate brain regions implicated in emotion regulation and stress response. By integrating mindfulness into daily routines and therapeutic interventions, caregivers and educators can empower children with invaluable skills for navigating the complexities of their inner worlds with grace and resilience.

1.3 How This Book Can Help

Against the backdrop of depression's pervasive impact on children's well-being, this book serves as a comprehensive resource for cultivating mindfulness skills tailored specifically to their needs. By providing a structured framework for understanding depression in children and integrating evidence-based mindfulness practices, this book equips caregivers, educators, and mental health professionals with the tools and insights necessary to support children on their journey toward healing. Through engaging activities, guided meditations, and practical strategies, this book empowers children to cultivate self-awareness, emotional resilience, and a sense of agency in navigating their mental health challenges. Furthermore, by fostering collaboration between caregivers, educators, and mental health professionals, this book facilitates a holistic approach to supporting children's mental health and well-being. Ultimately, "Mindfulness Skills for Kids with Depression" aspires to be more than a mere guidebook—it aims to be a catalyst for transformation, offering a beacon of hope and healing for children grappling with the shadows of depression.

In summation, the introduction sets the stage for a profound exploration of depression in children, the transformative potential of mindfulness, and the invaluable role of this book in supporting children's mental health and well-being. As we embark on this journey together, let us embrace compassion, curiosity, and resilience as guiding principles, illuminating the path toward healing and wholeness for our children and future generations.

2

What is mindfulness?

2.1 Defining Mindfulness for Kids

At its core, mindfulness can be understood as the practice of paying deliberate attention to the present moment without judgment. For children, mindfulness is about fostering awareness of their thoughts, feelings, bodily sensations, and surroundings in a non-judgmental manner. It encourages them to tune into their experiences with curiosity and acceptance, cultivating a deeper understanding of themselves and the world around them.

Mindfulness for kids often involves simple practices such as mindful breathing, where they focus on the sensation of their breath entering and leaving their bodies. It can also include activities like mindful eating, where they pay close attention to the taste, texture, and smell of their food. Additionally, mindfulness exercises for children may incorporate elements of movement, such as yoga or mindful walking, to promote body awareness and relaxation.

2.2 Benefits of Mindfulness Practice

The benefits of mindfulness practice for children are wide-ranging and profound. Firstly, it helps them develop emotional regulation skills by teaching them to recognize and manage their feelings more effectively. By learning to observe their emotions without immediately reacting to them, children can respond to challenging situations with greater resilience and clarity.

Moreover, mindfulness enhances attention and concentration, crucial skills for academic success and everyday life. By training their minds to focus on the present moment, children become better equipped to sustain attention, resist distractions, and engage more fully in tasks at hand.

Furthermore, mindfulness fosters self-awareness and empathy, enabling children to better understand their own needs and those of others. By cultivating a compassionate attitude towards themselves and their peers, children can build stronger relationships and contribute to a more harmonious social environment.

Additionally, research suggests that mindfulness practice can have tangible benefits for children's physical health, such as reducing stress levels, improving sleep quality, and strengthening immune function. By promoting relaxation and reducing the body's stress response, mindfulness contributes to overall well-being and resilience.

2.3 Myths and Misconceptions

Despite its growing popularity, mindfulness is sometimes subject to misconceptions that can hinder its adoption, especially among children. One common myth is that mindfulness requires clearing the mind of all thoughts, which can be intimidating and unrealistic, particularly for young minds. In reality, mindfulness is not about emptying the mind but rather observing thoughts as they arise without getting caught up in them.

Another misconception is that mindfulness is solely a relaxation technique. While mindfulness can induce feelings of calm and relaxation, its primary aim is to cultivate present-moment awareness and acceptance. It is not about escaping or avoiding difficult emotions but rather embracing them with openness and kindness.

Furthermore, some may believe that mindfulness is only suitable for certain personality types or religious affiliations. However, mindfulness is a secular practice that can benefit individuals of all ages, backgrounds, and beliefs. Its universal principles of awareness, acceptance, and compassion make it accessible to anyone seeking greater well-being and fulfillment.

In conclusion, mindfulness for kids offers a holistic approach to promoting mental, emotional, and physical well-being. By cultivating present-moment awareness, children can develop essential skills for navigating life's challenges with resilience, compassion, and clarity. It is essential to debunk common myths and misconceptions surrounding mindfulness to make this valuable practice more accessible and beneficial for children of all ages and backgrounds.

3

Getting Started with Mindfulness

Mindfulness, a practice rooted in ancient traditions such as Buddhism, has gained widespread recognition in recent years for its profound benefits on mental health and well-being. For children struggling with depression, cultivating mindfulness skills can be a powerful tool in managing symptoms and promoting emotional resilience. Getting started with mindfulness involves creating a safe and comfortable space, engaging in breathing exercises for beginners, and exploring mindful movement activities.

3.1 Creating a Safe and Comfortable Space

Establishing a conducive environment is essential for effective mindfulness practice, especially for children dealing with depression. The environment should be quiet, clutter-free, and free from distractions. Selecting an appropriate space, such as a corner of the child's room or a cozy spot in the living room, helps create a sense of sanctuary where the child can feel secure and at ease.

Ambiance plays a crucial role in setting the tone for mindfulness practice. Soft lighting, soothing colors, and comforting elements like pillows or blankets contribute to a calming atmosphere. Encouraging the child to personalize the space with items that evoke positive emotions or memories enhances their sense of connection and comfort.

Establishing ground rules for mindfulness sessions is also important. Children should be encouraged to respect the space and refrain from disruptive behavior. Emphasizing privacy and confidentiality allows the child to express themselves without fear of judgment or scrutiny.

Introducing sensory elements can further enhance the mindfulness experience. Soft background music, aromatherapy diffusers, or tactile objects like stress balls engage the senses and promote relaxation. By creating a safe and comfortable space, children can fully immerse themselves in mindfulness practice and reap its benefits.

3.2 Breathing Exercises for Beginners

Breathing exercises are fundamental to mindfulness practice, serving as an anchor for attention and promoting relaxation. For beginners, simple breathing exercises can be accessible and effective tools for cultivating mindfulness.

One such exercise is diaphragmatic breathing, also known as

"belly breathing." Encourage the child to find a comfortable seated position and place one hand on their abdomen. Instruct them to take slow, deep breaths through their nose, allowing their belly to rise like a balloon with each inhalation, and then exhale slowly through their mouth, feeling their belly deflate. Focusing on the sensation of their breath helps anchor their attention in the present moment and calms the mind.

Another beginner-friendly breathing exercise is "square breathing." Guide the child to inhale slowly for a count of four, hold their breath for a count of four, exhale for a count of four, and then hold their breath again for a count of four. This rhythmic pattern regulates breathing and induces a sense of calmness and balance.

3.3 Mindful Movement Activities

In addition to breathing exercises, incorporating mindful movement activities can further deepen mindfulness practice and promote physical well-being. Mindful movement encourages children to bring awareness to their bodies and movements, fostering a deeper connection between mind and body.

Yoga is a popular form of mindful movement that can be adapted for children of all ages and abilities. Simple yoga poses and stretches help release tension, improve flexibility, and promote relaxation. Child-friendly poses like downward-facing dog, cat-cow stretch, and child's pose introduce children to the benefits of yoga while fostering mindfulness and body awareness.

Walking meditation is another mindful movement activity that can be practiced indoors or outdoors. Encourage the child to walk slowly and deliberately, focusing on the sensations of their feet making contact with the ground, the rhythm of their footsteps, and the sights and sounds around them. Walking meditation cultivates mindfulness in everyday activities and promotes a sense of grounding and presence.

Incorporating mindful movement activities into daily routines empowers children to develop greater body awareness, improve coordination and balance, and enhance overall well-being. Encourage exploration and experimentation with different forms of movement, allowing children to discover activities that resonate with them and support their mindfulness journey.

In conclusion, getting started with mindfulness involves creating a safe and comfortable space, engaging in breathing exercises for beginners, and exploring mindful movement activities. By incorporating these practices into their daily lives, children can develop valuable skills for managing depression, promoting emotional well-being, and cultivating a deeper sense of presence and resilience.

4

Understanding Emotions in Children

Emotions are the cornerstone of human experience, shaping how we perceive and interact with the world around us. For children, emotions play a particularly vital role in their development, influencing their social relationships, academic performance, and overall well-being. In this comprehensive exploration of understanding emotions in children, we will delve deeper into the significance of emotional awareness, acceptance, and regulation, tailored specifically to the unique needs and experiences of young individuals.

4.1 Identifying Different Emotions

The journey of emotional intelligence begins with the ability to recognize and understand various emotions. For children, this process often starts in infancy, as caregivers help them decipher facial expressions, tone of voice, and body language to interpret their needs and feelings. As they grow and mature, children gradually learn to label their emotions and differentiate between different states of being.

Research suggests that children experience a wide range of emotions, including primary emotions such as joy, sadness, anger, fear, and disgust, as well as complex emotions like jealousy, guilt, and empathy. These emotions serve as vital signals that communicate important information about their internal states, desires, and experiences.

Encouraging children to identify and express their emotions fosters self-awareness and emotional literacy, empowering them to articulate their feelings effectively and seek appropriate support when needed. Through everyday interactions, care-givers can help children expand their emotional vocabulary by labeling emotions, validating experiences, and modeling healthy expressions of feelings.

4.2 Acceptance and Validation

In addition to identifying emotions, children need to learn that all emotions are valid and worthy of acknowledgment. Acceptance involves recognizing that emotions, whether positive or negative, are natural responses to internal and external stimuli and do not define a person's worth or identity. By embracing the full spectrum of emotions, children can cultivate a sense of self-compassion and acceptance, promoting emotional well-being and resilience.

Validation is another essential aspect of supporting children's emotional development. When caregivers validate children's emotions, they communicate empathy, understanding, and acceptance, which helps children feel seen, heard, and valued. Validating statements such as "I understand why you're feeling upset" or "It's okay to be afraid sometimes" validate children's experiences and provide reassurance that their feelings matter.

However, it's important for caregivers to distinguish between validating emotions and condoning inappropriate behaviors. While all emotions are valid, not all behaviors are acceptable. Caregivers can help children understand the difference by validating their feelings while also setting clear boundaries and teaching appropriate ways to express themselves constructively.

4.3 Coping Strategies for Emotional Regulation

Emotional regulation refers to the ability to manage and modulate one's emotional responses effectively. For children, developing healthy coping strategies is crucial for navigating the complexities of emotions and building resilience in the face of challenges. Here are some practical coping strategies that children can use to regulate their emotions:

1. Deep Breathing: Encourage children to practice deep breathing exercises when they feel overwhelmed or upset. Deep breathing helps activate the body's relaxation response, calming the nervous system and reducing stress levels.

2. Mindfulness Activities: Introduce children to mindfulness practices, such as meditation, guided imagery, or mindful breathing. Mindfulness cultivates present-moment awareness

and teaches children to observe their thoughts and emotions without judgment.

3. Expressive Arts: Engage children in creative activities, such as drawing, painting, or writing, to express their emotions in a safe and constructive manner. Artistic expression allows children to externalize their feelings and gain insight into their inner world.

4. Physical Activity: Encourage children to engage in regular physical exercise, such as dancing, jumping, or playing outside. Physical activity releases endorphins, neurotransmitters that promote feelings of happiness and well-being, while also providing a healthy outlet for pent-up emotions.

5. Social Support: Teach children the importance of seeking support from trusted adults, friends, or family members when they're struggling with difficult emotions. Building strong social connections fosters a sense of belonging and provides emotional validation and encouragement.

6. Positive Self-Talk: Help children develop positive self-talk habits by challenging negative thoughts and replacing them with affirming and empowering statements. Encourage them to cultivate a growth mindset and focus on their strengths and abilities.

By equipping children with a diverse toolbox of coping strategies, caregivers empower them to manage their emotions skillfully and navigate life's challenges with resilience and confidence. Through ongoing support, guidance, and validation, caregivers play a pivotal role in nurturing children's emotional intelligence and well-being.

In conclusion, understanding emotions in children is a multifaceted process that involves identifying, accepting, and regulating various emotional experiences. By fostering emotional awareness, acceptance, and coping skills, caregivers can help children develop the emotional intelligence necessary for navigating life's ups and downs with confidence and resilience.

5

Mindfulness in Daily Life

In today's fast-paced world, children are often bombarded with stimuli that can lead to stress, anxiety, and other mental health challenges. As parents, caregivers, and educators, it's crucial to equip kids with tools to navigate these pressures and cultivate a sense of inner peace and resilience. One such tool is mindfulness – the practice of being present in the moment with non-judgmental awareness. In this exploration, we delve into how mindfulness can be seamlessly woven into children's daily routines, focusing on bringing mindfulness into daily activities, mindful eating practices, and mindful communication with others.

5.1 Bringing Mindfulness into Daily Routines

Children's daily routines are filled with numerous activities, from waking up in the morning to going to bed at night. These routines provide ample opportunities to infuse mindfulness into their lives. For example, starting the day with a mindfulness ritual such as deep breathing exercises or a short guided meditation can set a positive tone for the day ahead. Encouraging kids to pay attention to their senses as they brush their teeth, take a shower, or get dressed can also foster mindfulness. By bringing awareness to each moment, children learn to appreciate the simple joys of everyday life and develop a greater sense of presence and calmness.

Furthermore, transitions between activities present opportune moments to practice mindfulness. For instance, before starting homework or chores, encourage kids to take a few mindful breaths to center themselves and shift their focus away from distractions. Similarly, incorporating mindfulness into bedtime routines can help children unwind and prepare for a restful night's sleep. Whether it's through guided relaxation exercises or practicing gratitude for the day's experiences, bedtime rituals can become sacred moments of reflection and peace.

5.2 Mindful Eating Practices

In today's fast-food culture, mindful eating is a valuable skill that can promote healthy habits and a positive relationship with food. For children, who may be easily distracted or prone to mindless snacking, cultivating mindful eating practices can foster greater awareness of their bodies' hunger and fullness cues, as well as appreciation for the taste, texture, and aroma of food.

One way to encourage mindful eating is to involve children in meal preparation. Engaging their senses as they wash, chop, and cook ingredients not only teaches valuable life skills but also fosters a deeper connection to the food they eat. During meals, encourage children to eat slowly, savoring each bite and noticing the flavors and textures. Encourage them to put down their utensils between bites, chew slowly, and pay attention to the sensations of hunger and fullness in their bodies.

Additionally, fostering a mindful eating environment free from distractions such as screens or electronic devices allows children to focus solely on the act of eating and the experience of nourishing their bodies. By teaching children to eat with intention and awareness, we empower them to make healthier food choices and develop a positive relationship with food that extends into adulthood.

5.3 Mindful Communication with Others

Effective communication is a cornerstone of healthy relationships, and mindfulness can enhance children's ability to communicate with clarity, empathy, and compassion. Mindful communication involves being fully present and attentive to both oneself and others during interactions, listening with an open mind, and responding thoughtfully rather than reactively.

One way to cultivate mindful communication skills in children is through activities that promote active listening and empathy. For example, engaging in mindful listening exercises where children pair up and take turns sharing their thoughts and feelings while the other practices attentive listening without interrupting or judging fosters empathy and understanding.

Furthermore, teaching children to pause and reflect before responding to others' words or actions can help them communicate more effectively and avoid impulsive or hurtful reactions. Encouraging them to use "I" statements to express their thoughts and feelings assertively while also respecting the perspectives of others promotes constructive dialogue and conflict resolution.

Moreover, modeling mindful communication in our own interactions with children – speaking calmly and respectfully, actively listening without distractions, and validating their feelings – sets a powerful example for them to emulate in their own relationships.

In conclusion, integrating mindfulness into children's daily lives offers a myriad of benefits, from promoting emotional regulation and stress reduction to fostering greater self-awareness and empathy. By incorporating mindfulness into daily routines, eating practices, and communication with others, we equip children with invaluable tools to navigate life's challenges with resilience, compassion, and presence. As caregivers and educators, let us nurture the seeds of mindfulness in the hearts and minds of our children, cultivating a brighter, more peaceful future for generations to come.

6

Cultivating Gratitude

Cultivating gratitude in children is a fundamental aspect of their emotional and mental well-being. Teaching kids to appreciate the good things in their lives fosters a positive outlook, resilience, and empathy. In this comprehensive exploration, we'll delve into various techniques tailored specifically for children to cultivate gratitude effectively.

6.1 Gratitude Journaling

Gratitude journaling is a simple yet powerful practice that encourages children to reflect on the positive aspects of their lives. Providing kids with a journal where they can regularly jot down things they are thankful for helps them develop a habit of gratitude. It could be anything from the love of their family and friends to the beauty of nature or even small everyday joys like a delicious meal or a sunny day.

To make gratitude journaling engaging for kids, encourage them to decorate their journals with colorful drawings or stickers that represent the things they are grateful for. Incorporating creative elements makes the practice more enjoyable and reinforces the habit. Additionally, you can guide them to write specific details about why they appreciate each thing, helping them deepen their understanding of gratitude.

6.2 Mindful Appreciation Exercises

Mindful appreciation exercises are another effective way to cultivate gratitude in children. These exercises involve encouraging kids to focus their attention on their senses and fully immerse themselves in the present moment. For example, you can guide them through a mindful walk in nature, asking them to notice the colors, sounds, and scents around them.

During the exercise, prompt children to express gratitude for the beauty and wonders of nature. Encourage them to pay attention to the intricate details of a flower, the soothing sound of birds chirping, or the gentle breeze against their skin. By teaching kids to appreciate the small moments of beauty in their surroundings, you help them develop a deeper sense of gratitude and connection to the world around them.

6.3 Acts of Kindness and Compassion

Encouraging children to perform acts of kindness and compassion is a powerful way to cultivate gratitude while also fostering empathy and altruism. Engage kids in activities that promote kindness towards others, such as volunteering at a local charity, helping a friend in need, or simply performing random acts of kindness in their daily lives.

Provide children with opportunities to experience the joy of giving and the impact of their actions on others. Encourage them to reflect on how their kindness makes a difference in someone else's life and how it feels to help others. By instilling a sense of empathy and compassion in children, you not only cultivate gratitude but also contribute to the development of their character and social skills.

Incorporating gratitude practices into children's lives has numerous benefits beyond just fostering a positive mindset. Research has shown that regularly practicing gratitude can improve children's overall well-being, enhance their relationships with others, and even boost their academic performance. By teaching kids to focus on the good things in their lives, you equip them with valuable coping skills that help them navigate challenges with resilience and optimism.

Moreover, gratitude serves as a powerful antidote to negative emotions such as envy, resentment, and entitlement. By shifting their focus from what they lack to what they have, children learn to cultivate a sense of abundance and appreciation for the blessings in their lives. This mindset not only promotes happiness and fulfillment but also helps children develop a more positive outlook on life.

In conclusion, cultivating gratitude in children is a transformative practice that has far-reaching benefits for their emotional, social, and cognitive development. By incorporating gratitude journaling, mindful appreciation exercises, and acts of kindness and compassion into their lives, you empower children to lead happier, more fulfilling lives and become compassionate, empathetic individuals who positively impact the world around them.

7

Managing Stress and Anxiety in Children

Stress and anxiety are common experiences for children as they navigate the challenges of growing up, facing academic pressures, social interactions, and other life changes. While some level of stress is normal and even beneficial for children's development, excessive or chronic stress can have detrimental effects on their mental and physical health. As caregivers and educators, it's crucial to recognize the signs of stress and anxiety in children, equip them with effective mindfulness techniques for stress reduction, and help them create a relaxation toolbox to manage their emotional well-being.

7.1 Recognizing Signs of Stress and Anxiety in Children

Children may express stress and anxiety in various ways, and it's essential to be attentive to their behaviors, emotions, and physical symptoms. Common signs of stress and anxiety in children include:

1. Behavioral Changes: Children may exhibit changes in behavior, such as irritability, mood swings, withdrawal from activities they used to enjoy, increased clinginess, or avoidance of certain situations.
2. Emotional Distress: They may experience frequent or intense feelings of worry, fear, nervousness, or sadness. They might also have difficulty concentrating or seem overwhelmed by simple tasks.
3. Physical Symptoms: Stress and anxiety can manifest in physical symptoms such as headaches, stomachaches, muscle tension, fatigue, difficulty sleeping, or changes in appetite.

It's essential to validate children's feelings and create a supportive environment where they feel comfortable expressing their emotions without judgment. Encourage open communication and provide reassurance that it's okay to feel stressed or anxious sometimes.

7.2 Mindfulness Techniques for Stress Reduction in Children

Mindfulness offers children valuable tools to manage stress and anxiety by cultivating present-moment awareness, acceptance, and self-compassion. Teaching mindfulness techniques to children can empower them to navigate challenging emotions and build resilience. Here are some mindfulness practices specifically tailored for children:

1. Mindful Breathing: Teach children simple breathing exer-

cises to anchor their attention to the present moment. For example, guide them to take slow, deep breaths, focusing on the sensation of air entering and leaving their nostrils or the rise and fall of their abdomen.

2. Body Scan: Lead children through a body scan practice where they systematically focus their attention on different parts of their body, noticing any tension or sensations without judgment. Encourage them to relax each body part as they breathe deeply.

3. Mindful Observation: Engage children in mindful observation activities, such as guided imagery or sensory awareness exercises. Encourage them to notice and describe their surroundings using their senses—what they see, hear, smell, taste, and touch—without labeling or analyzing.

By incorporating these mindfulness techniques into children's daily routines, whether at home or in school, they can develop a greater sense of emotional awareness and self-regulation.

7.3 Creating a Relaxation Toolbox for Children

A relaxation toolbox is a collection of strategies and resources that children can use to cope with stress and anxiety proactively. Encourage children to personalize their relaxation toolbox with activities and items that resonate with them. Here are some ideas to include in a relaxation toolbox for children:

1. Calming Activities: Provide calming activities such as coloring, drawing, or journaling, which can help children

express their emotions and relax their minds. Encourage them to engage in creative expression as a form of self-expression and stress relief.

2. Sensory Tools: Include sensory tools such as stress balls, fidget toys, or sensory bottles filled with glitter or sand. These tactile experiences can help children redirect their focus and regulate their emotions through sensory stimulation.

3. Relaxation Techniques: Teach children relaxation techniques such as progressive muscle relaxation or guided imagery. These techniques can help children release tension from their bodies and calm their minds by focusing on pleasant imagery or sensations.

Encourage children to use their relaxation toolbox whenever they feel stressed or overwhelmed, whether at home, school, or in other settings. Remind them that they have the power to choose how they respond to stressors and that taking proactive steps to care for their well-being is a sign of strength.

In conclusion, managing stress and anxiety in children requires a holistic approach that addresses their emotional, cognitive, and physical needs. By recognizing the signs of stress and anxiety, teaching mindfulness techniques for stress reduction, and helping children create a relaxation toolbox, caregivers and educators can empower children to develop resilience and thrive in the face of life's challenges. Let's prioritize children's mental health and well-being by providing them with the tools and support they need to navigate stress and anxiety with confidence and resilience.

8

Building Resilience

In the journey of childhood, encountering obstacles, setbacks, and challenges is inevitable. However, the ability to bounce back from adversity and develop resilience is crucial for the mental and emotional well-being of children, especially those dealing with depression. This chapter explains the vital aspects of building resilience in children through the lens of mindfulness.

8.1 Developing a Growth Mindset

A growth mindset is the belief that one's abilities and intelligence can be developed through dedication and hard work. It's about embracing challenges, persisting in the face of setbacks, and seeing effort as a path to mastery. For children struggling with depression, cultivating a growth mindset can be transformative.

Encouraging children to adopt a growth mindset involves praising their efforts and strategies rather than solely focusing on their achievements. By emphasizing the process of learning and improvement, children learn to see failures as opportunities for growth rather than reflections of their abilities. Mindfulness plays a pivotal role in nurturing a growth mindset by fostering self-awareness and self-compassion.

Mindfulness practices, such as mindful breathing and body scans, help children become aware of their thoughts and emotions without judgment. This awareness enables them to recognize negative thought patterns associated with fixed mindset beliefs and replace them with more adaptive and resilient thinking. Through mindfulness, children learn to view challenges as opportunities to learn and grow, cultivating perseverance and resilience along the way.

8.2 Overcoming Setbacks with Mindfulness

Setbacks and failures are an inevitable part of life, but they can be particularly challenging for children with depression. However, mindfulness equips children with the tools to navigate setbacks with resilience and grace. By cultivating present moment awareness and acceptance, children learn to respond to setbacks with clarity and resilience rather than reacting impulsively or becoming overwhelmed by negative emotions.

One powerful mindfulness practice for overcoming setbacks is RAIN: Recognize, Accept, Investigate, and Non-identification. When children encounter a setback, they can use the RAIN technique to approach the situation with mindfulness and compassion. First, they recognize and acknowledge their emotions without judgment. Then, they accept the reality of the situation and their feelings without resistance. Next, they investigate the underlying thoughts and beliefs contributing to their emotional reaction. Finally, they practice non-identification by recognizing that their thoughts and emotions do not define them.

Through the practice of RAIN and other mindfulness techniques, children learn to cultivate resilience in the face of setbacks by developing a greater sense of self-awareness, acceptance, and compassion. Instead of being consumed by negative thoughts and emotions, they learn to respond to challenges with resilience, adaptability, and a growth mindset.

8.3 Finding Strength in Adversity

Adversity is a natural part of life, but it can be particularly challenging for children struggling with depression. However, mindfulness offers a powerful framework for finding strength and resilience in the face of adversity. By cultivating present moment awareness and acceptance, children learn to navigate difficult situations with courage, compassion, and resilience.

One mindfulness practice for finding strength in adversity is the "anchor in the storm" meditation. In this practice, children visualize themselves as a sturdy anchor amidst a stormy sea of emotions and challenges. As they breathe deeply and ground themselves in the present moment, they cultivate a sense of stability, strength, and resilience in the face of adversity.

Additionally, mindfulness teaches children to approach adversity with an open heart and a compassionate attitude. By cultivating self-compassion and empathy, children learn to respond to challenges with kindness and understanding, both towards themselves and others. This compassionate approach to adversity fosters resilience by helping children develop a sense of inner strength and self-efficacy.

Overall, Chapter 8 of "Mindfulness Skills for Kids with Depression" highlights the importance of building resilience in children through mindfulness. By developing a growth mindset, overcoming setbacks with mindfulness, and finding strength in adversity, children can cultivate the resilience needed to navigate life's challenges with courage, compassion, and grace. Through the practice of mindfulness, children learn to embrace challenges as opportunities for growth and develop the inner resources needed to thrive in the face of adversity.

9

Connecting with Others

In the journey of aiding kids grappling with depression through mindfulness, Chapter 9 emerges as a pivotal juncture where we explore the significance of forging connections with others. Social interactions serve as linchpins in a child's mental well-being, especially amidst the throes of depression. This chapter intricately examines three foundational aspects: nurturing supportive relationships, honing mindful listening skills, and nurturing empathy and understanding.

9.1 Building Supportive Relationships

The cornerstone of resilience for children navigating the labyrinth of depression lies in the scaffolding of supportive relationships. A robust support system provides solace, validation, and a sanctuary of understanding, indispensable for their mental health. For children, these relationships often germinate within their familial orbit but can sprawl to encompass friendships, mentors, and trusted adults.

The cultivation of supportive relationships hinges upon sowing seeds of trust, fostering open channels of communication, and nurturing mutual respect. Parents and caregivers can sow the seeds of meaningful connections by carving out quality time, engaging in shared activities, and attuning to their child's thoughts and emotions sans judgment.

Moreover, it's imperative to illuminate the concept of healthy boundaries within relationships. Children must grasp that while it's commendable to seek solace and assistance when warranted, they are also entitled to demarcate boundaries to safeguard their well-being.

9.2 Mindful Listening Skills

Mindful listening, an invaluable tool in the arsenal of communication, serves to fortify bonds and enrich relationships. In the realm of depression, the gift of being truly heard and comprehended can metamorphose into a beacon of hope in a child's life. Mindful listening entails the art of being wholly present, attuned, and nonjudgmental whilst the other person articulates their thoughts.

Inculcating mindful listening skills in children commences with nurturing an awareness of their own ruminations and emotions. By acquainting them with the art of quelling the cacophony of internal dialogue and anchoring themselves in the present moment, children can hone the art of listening to others sans the interference of their internal monologue.

Furthermore, fostering active listening strategies, such as maintaining eye contact, nodding affirmatively, and paraphrasing the speaker's discourse, empowers children to exude empathy and convey their respect for the speaker's viewpoint. Encouraging them to pose open-ended queries and reflect upon their responses engenders a deeper comprehension and connection with their peers.

Furthermore, modeling mindful listening behaviors as adults can be a potent catalyst in nurturing these skills in children. When children witness adults actively listening and responding with empathy and compassion, they are more inclined to emulate these behaviors in their own interactions.

9.3 Empathy and Understanding

Empathy, the cornerstone of harmonious coexistence, epitomizes the ability to comprehend and resonate with the sentiments of others. It serves as a bedrock for fostering meaningful connections and nurturing supportive relationships. For children grappling with depression, the assurance that others can empathize with their plight can proffer a semblance of validation and solace.

Fostering empathy in children involves instilling an awareness of their own emotions and equipping them with the tools to discern and respond to the sentiments of others. This can be achieved through an array of activities such as storytelling, role-playing, and engaging in perspective-taking exercises.

Moreover, promoting acts of kindness and compassion fosters

empathy by sensitizing children to the trials and tribulations of others. By volunteering, extending a helping hand to those in need, and expressing gratitude, children imbibe the essence of empathy, forging bonds of solidarity and understanding.

Furthermore, fostering diversity and inclusivity in children's social circles can broaden their horizons and deepen their empathy. Encouraging interactions with peers hailing from diverse backgrounds and cultures fosters empathy, nurturing acceptance and appreciation for divergent perspectives and experiences.

In summation, Chapter 9 underscores the pivotal role of connecting with others in the journey of children grappling with depression. By nurturing supportive relationships, honing mindful listening skills, and fostering empathy and understanding, we sow the seeds of a nurturing milieu wherein children feel valued, heard, and buoyed in their odyssey towards healing and well-being.

10

Self-Compassion and Self-Care

In the journey of helping kids navigate through depression using mindfulness skills, Chapter 10 is a pivotal point. This chapter explores the crucial concepts of self-compassion and self-care, offering valuable insights and practical strategies tailored specifically for children.

10.1 Being Kind to Yourself

Self-compassion is the foundation upon which mental well-being is built. For kids grappling with depression, learning to be kind to themselves is an essential skill. Often, children experiencing depression can be overly critical of themselves, blaming themselves for their struggles or feeling inadequate compared to their peers. In this section, we explore ways to foster self-compassion in kids:

Teach self-compassionate language: Encourage children to

speak to themselves with kindness and understanding, just as they would to a friend in need. Phrases like "It's okay to make mistakes," "I'm doing my best," or "I am worthy of love and respect" can help cultivate a compassionate inner dialogue.

Practice self-acceptance: Help children recognize that they are valuable and deserving of love and respect, regardless of their perceived flaws or shortcomings. Encourage them to embrace their unique qualities and appreciate themselves for who they are.

Promote self-forgiveness: Guide children to acknowledge their mistakes and shortcomings without dwelling on self-blame or guilt. Teach them that making mistakes is a natural part of learning and growth, and that forgiveness, both for themselves and others, is an essential aspect of self-compassion.

10.2 Self-Care Activities for Kids

Self-care is not just a buzzword; it's a vital aspect of maintaining mental and emotional well-being for children. Engaging in regular self-care activities can help kids recharge, manage stress, and cultivate resilience in the face of depression. Here are some self-care activities tailored for children:

Mindful breathing exercises: Teach kids simple breathing techniques, such as deep belly breathing or square breathing, to help them calm their minds and bodies during times of stress or overwhelm.

Creative expression: Encourage children to express themselves creatively through art, music, writing, or other forms of self-expression. Creative activities can serve as outlets for emotions, allowing children to explore and process their feelings in a healthy way.

Physical activity: Promote regular physical activity as a means of promoting overall well-being. Whether it's going for a bike ride, playing a sport, or simply dancing around the living room, getting moving can help boost mood and reduce symptoms of depression.

Time in nature: Encourage children to spend time outdoors and connect with nature. Nature has a calming effect on the mind and body, reducing stress and promoting feelings of peace and relaxation.

10.3 Setting Healthy Boundaries

In the midst of dealing with depression, children may struggle with setting and maintaining healthy boundaries in their relationships and daily lives. Setting boundaries is essential for protecting one's mental and emotional well-being and fostering healthy relationships with others. Here are some strategies for teaching kids about setting healthy boundaries:

Identify personal boundaries: Help children identify their own needs, values, and limits. Encourage them to reflect on what feels comfortable and uncomfortable for them in various situations and relationships.

Communicate assertively: Teach children how to communicate

their boundaries assertively and respectfully to others. Encourage them to use "I" statements and express their needs and limits clearly and directly.

Practice self-advocacy: Empower children to advocate for themselves and their boundaries, even in the face of resistance or pushback from others. Help them understand that it's okay to prioritize their own well-being and assert their boundaries, even if it may be uncomfortable at times.

Model healthy boundaries: Lead by example and demonstrate healthy boundary-setting in your own interactions with your child and others. Show them that it's possible to assertively and respectfully communicate boundaries while maintaining positive relationships.

In conclusion, Chapter 10 of "Mindfulness Skills for Kids with Depression" explores the vital concepts of self-compassion, self-care, and setting healthy boundaries. By teaching children to be kind to themselves, engage in self-care activities, and assert their boundaries, we empower them to cultivate resilience, manage their depression, and thrive in their lives.

11

Mindful Problem-Solving

In the journey of helping kids with depression cultivate mindfulness skills, Chapter 11 serves as a pivotal guide in navigating the complexities of problem-solving. Titled "Mindful Problem-Solving," this chapter explores the intricacies of identifying problems, applying mindfulness-based strategies, and recognizing the importance of seeking help when needed. By fostering a mindful approach to problem-solving, children can develop resilience, confidence, and a sense of agency in managing challenges.

11.1 Identifying Problems and Challenges

The first step in effective problem-solving is recognizing and understanding the issues at hand. For children struggling with depression, identifying problems can be challenging, as the cloud of negative emotions may overshadow their ability to perceive situations objectively. In this section, we explore techniques to help kids pinpoint the root causes of their difficulties.

One approach is teaching children to practice mindfulness of their thoughts and emotions. By cultivating awareness of their internal experiences, kids can better discern the triggers and patterns contributing to their distress. Encourage them to engage in mindful reflection, perhaps through journaling or guided meditation, to explore their thoughts and feelings without judgment.

Additionally, fostering open communication is essential. Create a safe and supportive environment where children feel comfortable expressing their concerns and sharing their experiences. Encourage active listening and validate their emotions, reassuring them that their feelings are valid and worthy of attention.

Furthermore, guide children in identifying both internal and external challenges. Internal challenges may include negative self-talk, self-doubt, or perfectionism, while external challenges could involve academic stress, conflicts with peers, or family issues. By distinguishing between these different types of challenges, children can gain clarity on where to direct their problem-solving efforts.

11.2 Mindfulness-Based Problem-Solving Strategies

Once the problems have been identified, the next step is to explore mindfulness-based strategies for addressing them. Mindfulness empowers children to approach problems with a clear and focused mindset, enabling them to tap into their inner resources and creative problem-solving abilities.

One effective strategy is teaching children to practice mindful observation. Encourage them to step back and observe the situation from a detached perspective, like an impartial observer. By distancing themselves from the emotional intensity of the problem, children can gain a broader perspective and identify potential solutions more effectively.

Another valuable technique is mindfulness of emotions. Help children recognize how their emotions influence their perception of problems and their ability to find solutions. By learning to regulate their emotions through mindfulness practices such as deep breathing or progressive muscle relaxation, children can enhance their resilience and problem-solving skills.

Moreover, guide children in cultivating a growth mindset. Encourage them to view challenges as opportunities for growth and learning rather than insurmountable obstacles. Teach them to embrace setbacks with curiosity and resilience, knowing that each failure brings valuable lessons and insights.

Furthermore, encourage children to practice mindfulness in decision-making. Help them pause and reflect before making impulsive choices, guiding them to consider the potential consequences of their actions and the values they hold dear. By making decisions mindfully, children can align their actions with their long-term goals and aspirations.

11.3 Seeking Help When Needed

Despite their best efforts, children may encounter problems that are beyond their ability to solve independently. In such cases, it is essential to emphasize the importance of seeking help and support from trusted adults, peers, or mental health professionals.

Encourage children to reach out for help when they feel over-whelmed or stuck. Teach them to recognize the signs that indicate the need for assistance, such as persistent feelings of distress, difficulty coping with daily activities, or thoughts of self-harm. Emphasize that seeking help is a sign of strength, not weakness, and that there are people who care about their well-being and are willing to support them.

Furthermore, provide children with resources and guidance on where to seek help. This may include trusted adults such as parents, teachers, or school counselors, as well as mental health professionals such as therapists or psychologists. Ensure that children know how to access these resources and encourage them to reach out whenever they need support.

Mindful Problem-Solving equips children with the tools and strategies they need to navigate challenges with resilience and confidence. By fostering mindfulness in problem-solving, children can develop a deeper understanding of their difficulties, cultivate creative and effective solutions, and recognize the importance of seeking help when needed. Through mindfulness, children can build the resilience and self-efficacy they need to thrive in the face of adversity.

12

Mindfulness in School

This chapter focuses on three key aspects: integrating mindfulness practices into the classroom, fostering mindful study habits, and effectively managing academic pressure. In today's educational landscape, characterized by increasing demands and pressures, children encounter various stressors that can significantly impact their mental well-being. Thus, instilling mindfulness skills from an early age equips them with invaluable tools to navigate these challenges with resilience and self-awareness.

12.1 Bringing Mindfulness into the Classroom

Creating a conducive learning environment begins with introducing mindfulness practices into the classroom routine. Educators play a pivotal role in modeling and facilitating these practices, fostering a culture of mindfulness within the school community. By incorporating brief mindfulness exercises into daily activities, such as mindful breathing or grounding techniques, teachers help students cultivate focus, attention, and emotional regulation. These practices set the tone for a calm and supportive classroom atmosphere, conducive to effective learning and emotional well-being.

Furthermore, integrating mindfulness into lesson plans enhances student engagement and academic performance. Activities like mindful storytelling or mindful art encourage creativity and self-expression while promoting present-moment awareness. Moreover, incorporating mindfulness discussions cultivates empathy and enhances interpersonal relationships among students, fostering a sense of belonging and mutual respect within the classroom.

12.2 Mindful Study Habits

Developing effective study habits is crucial for academic success and overall well-being. Mindfulness-based study strategies empower students to approach learning with intentionality and focus. Educators can guide students in creating optimal study environments free from distractions, promoting concentration and productivity. Teaching time management techniques, such as the Pomodoro Technique or time-blocking, helps students manage their study sessions efficiently, preventing overwhelm and procrastination.

Encouraging active learning strategies, such as concept mapping or summarization, enhances comprehension and retention of information. Mindful reading practices, such as reflective reading or questioning, deepen students' engagement with course material, fostering critical thinking skills. Additionally, promoting self-awareness and self-reflection encourages students to identify their learning preferences and adjust their study strategies accordingly, maximizing learning outcomes.

12.3 Dealing with Academic Pressure

Navigating academic pressure is a significant challenge for many students, often leading to stress and anxiety. Mindfulness equips students with tools to manage academic pressure effectively and maintain well-being. Teaching stress-reduction techniques, such as mindful breathing or body scans, empowers students to regulate their emotions and stay grounded amidst academic demands.

Fostering a supportive classroom environment where students feel valued and encouraged promotes resilience and confidence in facing academic challenges. Emphasizing self-compassion and self-care reminds students to prioritize their mental and emotional well-being, fostering a healthy approach to academic success. Moreover, promoting a growth mindset encourages students to view setbacks as opportunities for learning and growth, cultivating resilience and perseverance.

By integrating mindfulness practices into the classroom, fostering mindful study habits, and teaching effective stress-management techniques, educators empower students to thrive academically and emotionally in today's demanding educational landscape.

13

Mindful Parenting and Family Support

This chapter aims to provide parents with practical strategies to support their child's mindfulness practice, implement mindful parenting techniques, and strengthen family bonds through mindfulness activities.

13.1 Supporting Your Child's Mindfulness Practice

Supporting your child's mindfulness practice involves creating an environment that encourages and nurtures their exploration of mindfulness techniques. As a parent, you can lead by example, integrating mindfulness into your own daily routine. This might involve practicing mindful breathing exercises, taking mindful walks together, or simply modeling present-moment awareness in everyday activities.

Encourage open communication with your child about their mindfulness practice. Listen to their experiences, validate their feelings, and offer gentle guidance when needed. Remember that mindfulness is a personal journey, and each child may have different preferences for mindfulness activities. Allow your child the autonomy to explore various techniques and find what resonates best with them.

Incorporate mindfulness into your child's daily routine by setting aside dedicated time for mindfulness practice. This could be a few minutes in the morning or before bedtime, providing a consistent opportunity for your child to engage in mindfulness exercises. Create a designated space in your home where your child feels comfortable practicing mindfulness, free from distractions.

Additionally, consider exploring mindfulness resources specifically designed for children, such as guided meditation apps, children's mindfulness books, or online mindfulness courses tailored to their age group. These resources can enhance your child's understanding of mindfulness and provide them with additional support outside of the home environment.

13.2 Mindful Parenting Techniques

Mindful parenting involves cultivating awareness, compassion, and non-judgmental acceptance in your interactions with your child. It requires being fully present and attuned to your child's needs, emotions, and experiences. Practicing mindful parenting techniques can create a nurturing and supportive environment that fosters your child's emotional well-being.

Start by practicing mindful listening during your interactions with your child. This means giving your child your full attention without judgment or distraction. Listen to their thoughts, feelings, and concerns with empathy and understanding, creating a safe space for them to express themselves openly.

Practice patience and acceptance in moments of difficulty or conflict. Instead of reacting impulsively, take a moment to pause and respond mindfully. Validate your child's emotions and help them navigate challenging situations with kindness and compassion.

Set boundaries and discipline with mindfulness, focusing on teaching lessons rather than punishing mistakes. Use positive reinforcement and encouragement to reinforce desired behaviors, and approach discipline with an emphasis on learning and growth.

Cultivate a sense of gratitude and appreciation within your family by engaging in mindful activities together. Practice gratitude exercises, such as keeping a gratitude journal or expressing appreciation for one another during family meals. These practices can foster a sense of connection and strengthen family bonds.

13.3 Strengthening Family Bonds through Mindfulness

Mindfulness offers a powerful tool for strengthening family bonds and fostering a sense of connection and unity. By engaging in mindfulness activities together, families can cultivate a deeper understanding and appreciation for one another.

Schedule regular family mindfulness sessions where you engage in mindfulness exercises as a group. This could include guided meditation, mindful breathing exercises, or mindful movement activities such as yoga or tai chi. These shared experiences can promote feelings of closeness and create cherished memories for your family.

Practice mindful communication within your family by actively listening to one another, speaking with kindness and compassion, and resolving conflicts peacefully. Encourage open dialogue and expression of emotions, creating a supportive environment where family members feel heard and valued.

Incorporate mindfulness into everyday family activities, such as mealtime, chores, or outdoor outings. Encourage mindfulness in simple moments, such as savoring a meal together without distractions or taking a mindful nature walk as a family.

Create rituals and traditions centered around mindfulness, such as a weekly family gratitude circle or a mindfulness-themed family movie night. These rituals can strengthen family bonds and provide opportunities for meaningful connection and reflection.

Overall, Chapter 13 emphasizes the importance of mindful parenting and family support in promoting the well-being of children with depression. By supporting your child's mindfulness practice, implementing mindful parenting techniques, and engaging in mindfulness activities as a family, you can create a nurturing and supportive environment that fosters resilience, emotional regulation, and positive mental health outcomes for your child.

14

Overcoming obstacles

This chapter acknowledges that despite the numerous benefits of mindfulness, children may face resistance, challenges, and difficulties in maintaining consistency and motivation. Therefore, it provides strategies and techniques tailored to help children navigate these obstacles effectively.

14.1 Dealing with Resistance to Mindfulness

Resistance to mindfulness can manifest in various forms among children. Some may express skepticism or disinterest in mindfulness practices, while others may actively resist participating in mindfulness activities. It's essential to understand the root causes of this resistance to address it effectively.

One common reason for resistance is the misconception that mindfulness is boring or difficult. Children may perceive mindfulness as sitting still for long periods or engaging in complex meditation practices. To overcome this resistance, it's crucial to introduce mindfulness in a fun and engaging way. Incorporating games, storytelling, and creative activities can make mindfulness more appealing to children.

Another factor contributing to resistance is a lack of understanding of the benefits of mindfulness. Children may not see how mindfulness can help them manage their emotions, reduce stress, and improve their overall well-being. Educating children about the positive effects of mindfulness through age-appropriate explanations and real-life examples can help alleviate resistance.

Additionally, some children may resist mindfulness due to underlying emotional or behavioral issues. For example, children with anxiety may find it challenging to sit still and focus on their breath, while children with ADHD may struggle with sustained attention during mindfulness practices. In such cases, it's essential to modify mindfulness techniques to suit the child's individual needs and abilities.

14.2 Addressing Common Challenges

Several common challenges may arise when children practice mindfulness. These challenges can hinder their progress and discourage them from continuing their mindfulness journey. By addressing these challenges proactively, children can develop resilience and perseverance in their mindfulness practice.

One common challenge is maintaining focus and attention during mindfulness activities. Children may find it difficult to quiet their minds and stay present, especially if they're accustomed to constant stimulation from screens and other distractions. To address this challenge, it's essential to start with short, simple mindfulness exercises and gradually increase the duration as children build their attention skills. Providing visual aids, such as guided imagery or mindfulness apps designed for kids, can also help children stay engaged.

Another challenge is dealing with difficult emotions that arise during mindfulness practice. Children may experience feelings of boredom, frustration, or discomfort when confronting their thoughts and emotions. It's essential to create a supportive and non-judgmental environment where children feel safe expressing their emotions. Teaching children self-compassion and acceptance can help them navigate challenging emotions with greater ease.

Furthermore, children may encounter logistical challenges, such as finding time to practice mindfulness amidst their busy schedules or dealing with distractions in their environment. Encouraging consistency and setting realistic expectations can help children overcome these challenges. Integrating mindfulness into daily routines, such as before bedtime or during transitions, can make it easier for children to incorporate mindfulness into their lives.

14.3 Maintaining Consistency and Motivation

Consistency and motivation are key factors in establishing a sustainable mindfulness practice. However, children may struggle to maintain consistency due to competing priorities, lack of interest, or difficulty forming new habits. Therefore, it's essential to cultivate a supportive environment that fosters consistency and motivation.

One strategy for maintaining consistency is to create a routine around mindfulness practice. Consistency is reinforced when mindfulness becomes a regular part of a child's daily or weekly schedule. Designating specific times and places for mindfulness activities can help children develop a sense of routine and structure.

Another approach is to make mindfulness practice enjoyable and rewarding for children. Incorporating elements of play, creativity, and exploration into mindfulness activities can make them more engaging and motivating. Additionally, celebrating small victories and progress can boost children's confidence and enthusiasm for mindfulness.

Moreover, fostering a sense of community and connection can enhance children's motivation to practice mindfulness. Encouraging peer support and collaboration, such as practicing mindfulness with friends or participating in group activities, can create a sense of belonging and accountability. Recognizing and celebrating each other's efforts can further strengthen children's commitment to mindfulness.

By addressing resistance, addressing common challenges, and maintaining consistency and motivation, children can develop the skills and resilience needed to reap the benefits of mindfulness and improve their mental health and well-being.

15

Moving Forward

In the journey towards healing and managing depression, moving forward is a crucial step for children. This chapter serves as a guide to celebrating progress and growth, setting mindful intentions for the future, exploring resources for continued practice, and concluding the mindfulness journey.

15.1 Celebrating Progress and Growth

Recognizing and celebrating progress and growth are pivotal aspects of a child's journey in battling depression. It's imperative to acknowledge even the smallest steps forward. Whether it's completing a mindfulness exercise without distraction or expressing emotions more openly, every achievement holds significance. Celebrating progress not only boosts self-esteem but also reinforces the idea that change is possible.

Parents and caregivers play a crucial role in celebrating these milestones. Their support, praise, and encouragement are invaluable to the child's progress. Additionally, creating a tangible representation of progress, such as a mindfulness journal or a progress chart, can serve as a visual reminder of the strides made. Such visual aids can also help children recognize patterns in their behavior and emotions, empowering them to navigate their journey more effectively.

15.2 Setting Mindful Intentions for the Future

Setting mindful intentions involves cultivating awareness and directing one's actions towards positive outcomes. For children grappling with depression, setting intentions can foster a sense of control and empowerment over their mental health journey.

Encourage children to reflect on their values, interests, and aspirations. What do they hope to achieve in terms of their emotional well-being? Are there specific mindfulness practices they wish to incorporate into their daily routine? By identifying these intentions, children can create a roadmap for their future growth and development.

It's essential to emphasize the importance of setting realistic and achievable goals. Rather than solely focusing on outcomes, encourage children to embrace the process of self-discovery and self-improvement. Mindful intentions should be flexible and adaptable, allowing room for learning and growth along the way.

15.3 Resources for Continued Practice

Maintaining a regular mindfulness practice is fundamental to long-term well-being. In this section, explore various resources that children can utilize to continue their mindfulness journey beyond the pages of the book.

Online platforms and mobile applications offer a plethora of guided meditations, breathing exercises, and mindfulness activities tailored specifically for children. Encourage children to explore these resources and identify ones that resonate with them. Additionally, consider recommending books, podcasts, or workshops that delve deeper into mindfulness practices for kids.

Community-based programs and support groups also provide valuable opportunities for children to connect with others facing similar challenges. Whether it's joining a mindfulness club at school or participating in a local meditation group, these communal settings offer support, encouragement, and a sense of belonging.

15.4 Conclusion

In conclusion, "Mindfulness Skills for Kids with Depression" serves as a comprehensive guide to helping children cultivate mindfulness as a tool for managing depression and promoting emotional well-being. By celebrating progress and growth, setting mindful intentions for the future, exploring resources for continued practice, and concluding the mindfulness journey, children can embark on a path towards healing and resilience.

As children navigate life's ups and downs, mindfulness serves as a steadfast anchor, providing them with the tools and techniques needed to navigate challenges with greater ease and resilience. With continued practice and support, children can harness the power of mindfulness to cultivate a deeper sense of self-awareness, compassion, and inner peace.